Traverse Theatre Company

STILL

Frances Poet

Commissioned by the Traverse Theatre Company and
the Institute for Advanced Studies in the Humanities (IASH),
The University of Edinburgh.

First performed at the Traverse Theatre, Edinburgh,
on 2 August 2021.

Company List

Cast
DOUGIE	Martin Donaghy
GAYNOR	Molly Innes
MUSICIAN/BARTENDER	Oğuz Kaplangi
MICK	Gerry Mulgrew
CIARA	Mercy Ojelade
GILLY	Naomi Stirrat

Creative Team
Writer	Frances Poet
Director	Gareth Nicholls
Designer	Karen Tennent
Lighting Designer	Colin Grenfell
Composer & Sound Designer	Oğuz Kaplangi
Movement Director	Kally Lloyd-Jones
Dramaturg	Eleanor White
Associate Director	Shilpa T-Hyland

Production Team
Production Manager	Kevin McCallum
Chief Electrician	Renny Robertson
Head of Stage	Gary Staerck
Company Stage Manager	Owen Thomas
Deputy Stage Manager	Naomi Stalker
Costume Supervisor & Maintenance	Sophie Ferguson
Assistant Stage Manager	Katrina McMillan
Assistant Stage Manager	Rebecca Mitchell

Company Biographies

Martin Donaghy (DOUGIE)

Martin trained at the Royal Conservatoire of Scotland.

Theatre credits include: *The Panopticon* (National Theatre of Scotland); *Anything That Gives Off Light* (National Theatre of Scotland/Public Theatre NYC); *Losing the Rag* (A Play, A Pie and A Pint, Òran Mór); *549: Scots of the Spanish Civil War* (Wonder Fools/Glasgow Citizens Theatre); *Faithful Ruslan, The Story of a Guard Dog* (Belgrade Coventry/Glasgow Citizens Theatre); *Ring Road* (Traverse Theatre Company/A Play, A Pie and A Pint, Òran Mór); *Feverdream: Southside, Rum and Vodka, A Christmas Carol* and *Hamlet* (Citizens Theatre); *A Midsummer Night's Dream* (Bard in the Botanics); *Macbeth* (Southwark Playhouse); *Rudolph* (Platform Glasgow).

Screen credits include: *Outlander* Seasons 4 and 5 (Sony/Starz/Leftbank); *Repression* (Accento Films); *Beats* (Sixteen Films); *The Secret Agent* (BBC).

Colin Grenfell (Lighting Designer)

Work for Traverse Theatre Company Includes: *The Devil Masters, Pandas, On the Exhale* (China Plate). Other work includes: *The King of Hell's Palace* (Hampstead Theatre); *Gypsy, Macbeth, The Cherry Orchard, Kes* (Royal Exchange Theatre, Manchester); Tao of Glass (Manchester International Festival); *Still No Idea* (Improbable); *A Christmas Carol* (Everyman Liverpool, Spymokey) *Tamburlaine* (RSC); *The Mentor* (Theatre Royal Bath & Vaudeville Theatre); *Lost Without Words, Lifegame, Theatre of Blood* (Improbable/Royal National Theatre); *Black Watch, 365, Men Should Weep, The Bacchae, Granite* (National Theatre of Scotland); *The Village Social* (National Theatre of Wales); *Beauty and the Beast* (MCA, Chicago, Abrons New York, Adelaide Festival); *The Caretaker* (Liverpool Everyman, Trafalgar Studios, BAM); *A Midsummer Night's Dream, Half Life, The Mother, Forever Yours, Marie-Lou, Wild Goose Dreams, Xmas Eve* (Theatre Royal Bath); *70 Hill Lane, Coma, The Paper Man, Spirit* (Improbable); *Cat on a Hot Tin Roof* (Theatr Clwyd; Best Lighting Award at the 2017 Wales Theatre Awards); *The Elephant Man* (Best Design CATS award); *The Hanging Man* (Best Design TMA Awards).

Molly Innes (GAYNOR)

Work for Traverse Theatre Company includes: *The Artist Man and the Mother Woman, The Found Man, One Day All This Will Come to Nothing, Green Field, The Slab Boys Trilogy, A Solemn Mass for a Full Moon in Summer, Widows, Shining Souls, Stones and Ashes.*

Other work includes: *27, Rupture* (National Theatre of Scotland); *Thon Man Moliere, The Guid Sisters, Takin' Over the Asylum, The Marriage of Figaro, Wondrous Fitting, Pinocchio, Faust Part 1 & 2, To Kill a Mockingbird, The Prime of Miss Jean Brodie* (Royal Lyceum Theatre, Edinburgh); *Threads, Dare to Care, Age of Arousal, The Memory of Water, Wit* (Stellar Quines); *Into That Darkness* (Citizens Theatre); *Sleeping Queen* (King's Theatre, Glasgow); *Great Expectations* (Perth Theatre); *Timeless* (Suspect Culture); *Tartuffe* (Dundee Rep); *Good Things* (Borderline Theatre/Byre Theatre/Perth Rep); *Playboy of the Western World* (Communicado); *Plasticine* (Royal Court Theatre).

TV credits include: *The Nest, River City, Holby City, Rebus, Life Support, A Mug's Game, Strathblair, The Ferguson Theory, Rab C Nesbitt, Takin' Over the Asylum* (BBC); *Lovesick, Psychos* (Channel 4); *Taggart* (STV); *The Bill* (ITV) and numerous radio plays for BBC.

Film credits include: *Afterlife, Ratcatcher, Stella Does Tricks, Karmic Mothers.*

Molly received a Best Actress Commendation at the Ian Charleson/National Theatre Awards for *Electra* (Theatre Babel), a Critics' Award for Theatre in Scotland nomination for *All Day This Will Come to Nothing* (Traverse Theatre Company) and was nominated Best Actress at the Stage Awards for *Moving Objects* (Brunton Theatre).

Oğuz Kaplangi (Composer & Sound Designer)

Oğuz Kaplangi is a Turkish composer and sound designer based in Edinburgh, who primarily works in theatre, TV, film and advertising.

Oğuz moved to the UK in 2018 and that same year he was awarded with the 'Best Music and Sound' award at the Critics' Awards for Theatre in Scotland for the music he composed for Zinnie Harris's adaptation of Ionesco's play, *Rhinoceros.*

Oğuz has scored music for fifteen feature films, including box-office hits, and written music for US TV shows, including A&E's Emmy-nominated *Wahlburgers.* Oğuz's recent UK film credits include two short films and a feature. In both *A Glimpse* (recipient of Best Short Drama Award – SMHAF21) directed by Zinnie Harris, and *Last Summer* (Feature Film – Netflix) directed by Ozan Açıktan, Oğuz is credited as a composer. In Simone Lahbib's short film, *Swipe Right*, Oğuz has worked as a sound designer. Oğuz was selected as a creative member for BFI Network x BAFTA Crew 2021 Programme.

For the past 20 years, Oğuz has been writing music for ad agencies such as CP+B London, Wieden+Kennedy Amsterdam, and Ogilvy & Mather, Leo Burnett, DDB, BBDO, Saatchi & Saatchi, Thompson, MullenLowe, McCann Erickson, and 4129Grey in Istanbul.

Oğuz has released soundtracks as a solo artist, collaborated with international musicians and produced various World Music albums including the ethnic-electronic *Istanbul Calling* series.

For the Traverse Theatre Company: *Rabbit Catcher, Doomsdays, The Monstrous Heart.* Other theatre credits include: *Lyceum Christmas Tales, Tiny Tim, Nyanya and the Mighty Wizz!, Mrs Puntila and Her Man Matti* (Royal Lyceum Theatre); *A Museum in Baghdad, #WeAreArrested* (Royal Shakespeare Company); *The Alchemist* (Tron Theatre); *The Duchess [of Malfi]* (Royal Lyceum Theatre, Citizens Theatre); *Let the Right One In, Incendies, How to Hold Your Breath, Frozen, 0/Damage, Inc.* (DOT Theatre); *Rhinoceros* (Royal Lyceum Theatre, Edinburgh International Festival, DOT Theatre); *Meet Me at Dawn* (DOT Theatre, Arcola Theatre).

Kally Lloyd-Jones (Movement Director)

Kally Lloyd-Jones trained as a dancer and has an MA in English Literature and Film Studies from Glasgow University. She has worked in dance, opera and theatre, from small to large scale environments as director, producer, choreographer, movement director and teacher, with her own company as well as a number of other companies, both in the UK and internationally.

She has directed productions for Scottish Opera, The Royal Conservatoire of Scotland, St Andrews Opera, The Byre and Tête à Tête Opera, with movement directing across genres for Citizens Theatre, Royal Lyceum Theatre Edinburgh, Tron Theatre, Welsh National Opera, Royal Conservatoire of Scotland, Scottish Opera, Royal Swedish Opera, Danish National Opera and Glyndebourne. She is founder and Artistic Director of Company Chordelia and has created, directed and choreographed the company's award-winning productions, including *Lady Macbeth: Unsex Me Here, Nijinsky's Last Jump, Dance Derby, The Seven Deadly Sins* and *The Chosen*.

Since 2019, alongside Jessica Richards, Kally has been Joint Director of The Byre Theatre in St Andrews.

Gerry Mulgrew (MICK)

Gerry was awarded Best Male Performance at the Critics' Awards for Theatre in Scotland in 2007 for his role as Old Peer in *Peer Gynt* (Dundee Rep and National Theatre of Scotland).

For the Traverse Theatre Company: *Nova Scotia, Tree of Knowledge*. Other theatre credits include: *Ma, Pa and the Little Mouths* (Tron Theatre); Lost at Sea (Perth Theatre); *Krapp's Last Tape* (Tron Theatre/Blood of the Young); *Losing the Rag, The Last Dictator, The Above, Federer vs Murray* (A Play, A Pie and A Pint, Òran Mór); *Ay! Carmela!* (Out of the Box); *My Name is Ben, The Visit, Ubu the King* (Dundee Rep); *Peer Gynt* (Dundee Rep/National Theatre of Scotland); *Waiting for Godot* (Citizens Theatre); *Lanark* (Citizens Theatre/ Edinburgh International Festival); *Ane Satyre of the Three Estates* (Staging for the Scottish Court).

Gerry is a founding member and Artistic Director of Communicado Theatre Company, where his directing credits include: *The Government Inspector, The Memorandum, The Suicide, Blood Wedding, Cyrano de Bergerac, The Cone Gatherers, Mary Queen of Scots, Carmen, The Hunchback of Notre Dame* and *The House with the Green Shutters*.

Screen credits include: *River City* (BBC).

Short films include: *High Man Pen Meander* (Tron Theatre) and *Scenes for Survival: The Maid's Room* (National Theatre of Scotland).

Gareth Nicholls (Director)

Gareth joined the Traverse in May 2017 as its Associate Director before becoming Interim Artistic Director in late 2018, and Artistic Director in 2020. For the Traverse Theatre Company he has directed the award-winning Festival production, *Ulster American* by David Ireland, as well as the world premieres of *Crocodile Fever* by Meghan Tyler, Oliver Emanuel's *The Monstrous Heart* (in co-production with Stephen Joseph Theatre), Gary McNair's *Letters to Morrissey*, Morna Pearson's *How to Disappear* and Clare Duffy's *Arctic Oil*. In 2020 he adapted the stage production of Gary McNair's *A Gambler's Guide to Dying* for digital channels for the Traverse.

Previously he held the post of Citizens Theatre's Main Stage Director in Residence (2014–16), where his shows included *Into That Darkness*, *Vanya*, *Blackbird*, and the sell-out production of Irvine Welsh's *Trainspotting*.

Other directing credits include: the Scottish premiere of Yasmina Reza's *God of Carnage*, *Under Milk Wood* by Dylan Thomas (Tron Theatre); *Donald Robertson is Not a Stand-Up Comedian*, *A Gambler's Guide to Dying* by Gary McNair (Show & Tell); *Voices From the Black That I Am* by Karl O'Brian Williams, *Moby Dick* by Herman Melville and *Prom* by Oliver Emanuel (A Play, A Pie and A Pint, Òran Mór); *Educating Ronnie* by Joe Douglas (Utter/High Tide); *The Little Lost Boy That Santa Clause Forgot* (Macrobert Arts Centre); *The Tin Forest South West* (National Theatre of Scotland); *'Tis A Pity She's a Whore*, *Coriolanus*, *The Burial at Thebes* (Royal Conservatoire of Scotland).

His 2018 Festival production, *Ulster American*, won several awards including the Carol Tambor Best of Edinburgh Award. It went on to tour internationally and gained three Critics' Awards for Theatre in Scotland 2019 – Best New Play, Best Female Performance and Best Production.

Gareth has also won four Fringe First Awards (*Ulster American*, *Letters to Morrissey*, *Educating Ronnie* and *A Gambler's Guide to Dying*) and a Scottish Arts Club Award (*Donald Robertson is Not A Stand-Up Comedian*).

Mercy Ojelade (CIARA)

For Maria. x

Theatre credits include: *Season's Greetings* (Stephen Joseph Theatre); *Operation Black Antler* (Blast Theory/Hydrocracker/Southbank Centre); *Love and Information* (Sheffield Crucible Studio); *Richard III* (Perth Theatre); *The White Devil* (Sam Wanamaker Playhouse, Shakespeare's Globe); *They Drink it in the Congo* (Almeida Theatre); *A Midsummer Night's Dream: A Play for the Nation* (Royal Shakespeare Company); *Last Dream on Earth* (National Theatre of Scotland); *Tomorrow* (Vanishing Point Theatre); *Horizontal Collaboration* (Fire Exit); *Arabian Nights* (Tricycle Theatre); *Crash of the Elysium* (Punchdrunk/ BBC/Manchester International Festival); *Roadkill* (UK/US and Théâtre de la Ville); *How to Think the Unthinkable, The Man with the Disturbingly Smelly Foot* (Unicorn Theatre); *The Container* (Young Vic/ Edinburgh International Festival); *The Walworth Farce* (Druid Theatre, Ireland, National Theatre and world tour); *The Lion and the Jewel* (Barbican/UK tour) and *Eclipse* (Sydney Opera House Studio).

Film credits include: *Ezra, Incendiary*.

Television credits include: *EastEnders, Doctors, Holby City* (BBC); *Ørnen* (Denmark – DR); *Outlander* (Left Bank Pictures).

Radio credits include: *The Container* (BBC Radio Scotland).

Frances Poet (Writer)

Frances Poet is a Glasgow based writer. Her stage plays have been produced nationally and internationally and include *Maggie May* (Leeds Playhouse/ Leicester Curve/Queens Theatre, Hornchurch), *Crusaders* (NT Connections), *Fibres* (Stella Quines/Citizens Theatre), *Gut* (Traverse Theatre Company), also in a French translation as *Madra*, (Théâtre La Licorne) and *Adam* (National Theatre of Scotland).

Frances has also completed a number of classic adaptations including *The Macbeths* (Citizens Theatre); *What Put the Blood* (Abbey Theatre; and previously as Andromaque, Oran Mòr); *Dance of Death* (Candice Edmunds/Citizens Theatre) and *The Misanthrope* (Oran Mòr).

Radio work includes: *Alt Delete* (BBC Radio 3); *Gut* (BBC Radio 4) and *The Disappointed* (BBC Radio Scotland).

Screen work includes: Episode 5 of a new Scotland-set crime drama, *Annika*, several episodes of *River City* and short films that have played at a number of national and international festivals.

Awards and nominations include Susan Smith Blackburn Finalist (*Maggie May*), Writers' Guild Best Play Winner (*Gut*), Fringe First (*Adam*), Scottish Arts Club 'Flying Artichoke' Winner (*Adam*), Amnesty International Expression Of Freedom Award Nomination (*Adam*), UK Theatre Best Play Award Nomination (*Gut*) and Bruntwood Prize for Playwriting Shortlist (*Gut*).

Frances's play, *Sophia*, about the first woman doctor in Scotland, Sophia Jex Blake, will be presented as part of Pitlochry/Royal Lyceum Theatre Edinburgh, Sound Stage and available to listen to at the end of August.

Naomi Stirrat (GILLY)

Since graduating from Queen Margaret and Edinburgh Napier Universities, Naomi has worked on various productions and developments including: *Fallen Angel* (Sara and Giles); *Fallen Angels of the Moine, The Stornoway Way* (Dogstar); *UnTangled* (Make Do and Mend); *Which Wire's What* (Imaginate).

Screen credits include: *Annika* (Black Camel Pictures); *Eminent Monsters* (BBC); *And Repeat* (Little Viking).

Naomi is also part of the modern Scottish folk band, Celtic Worship.

Karen Tennent (Designer)

Karen is based in Edinburgh, Scotland, and is a graduate of Edinburgh College of Art. Her work as a theatre designer has toured all over the UK and abroad from village halls to Sydney Opera House. Her designs range from small scale tours to large scale installations.

Recent designs include: *Field – Something for the Future Now, Little by Little Field, ChalkAbout, Teenage Trilogy* (Curious Seed); *We Are All Just Little Creatures* (Lunga Ha/Curious Seed); *The Secret Garden* (Red Bridge Arts); *Lost at Sea* (Perth Theatre); *First Snow* (National Theatre of Scotland/Theatre PAP/Montreal); *Lots Not Lots* (National Theatre Scotland); *Strange Tales, Light Boxes* (Grid Iron/Traverse Theatre Company); *Glory on Earth, The Iliad, Caucasian Chalk Circle* (Royal Lyceum, Edinburgh); *Hansel and Gretel, Martha, Emma and Gill, The Voice Thief, Lifeboat, Eddie and the Slumber Sisters* (Catherine Wheels); *Lost in Music* (Magnetic North); *Our Fathers* (Magnetic North/Traverse Theatre Company); *Crumbles Search for Christmas, Flat Stanley* (West Yorkshire Playhouse); *God of Carnage, This Wide Night* (Tron Theatre); *ThingammyBob, The Three Sisters* (Lung Ha); *Expensive Shit* (Scottish Theatre Producers/Traverse Theatre Company); *A Game of Death and Chance, Enlightenment House* (National Trust for Scotland).

Past designs include: *The Suicide, Portrait of a Woman, Tall Tales for Small People, Arabian Nights, Playboy of the Western World, Place with the Pigs, The Memorandum* (Communicado); *Moby Dick* (Royal Shakespeare Company); *Good Things, Trelawny of the Wells* (Pitlochry Theatre); *Cinderella, Beauty and the Beast, Aladdin, Babes in the Wood, The Little Mermaid* (Macrobert Stirling); *Comic Potential, Marys Wedding, The Twits, Mother Goose, Cinderella* (Byre Theatre); *The Jungle Book, Hard Times, Flora the Red Menace* (Dundee Rep); *Flat Stanley, Paddington, The Jolly Postman, The Ugly Duckling, The Little Mermaid* (Polka Theatre); *The Red Balloon* (Visible Fictions).

Dance credits include: *Found, Push, The Woman Who Wants to be Funny, Code Butterfly, Threads* (Curious Seed); *Wee Home from Home, Double Helix, Parallel Parallels* (Plan B); *The Ancient Mariner* (Tabla Rasa); *Go Get 'em Kids* (Tamsin Russell); *Without a Hitch* (Room to Manoeuvre).

Karen also co-directed *Sonata for a Man and a Boy* (Greg Sinclair), winner of the Critics' Awards for Theatre in Scotland for Best Children's Theatre in 2013. Other directing credits include: *The Lion of Kabul* and *Stuck* (Catherine Wheels). She also won Best Design at the Critics' Awards for Theatre in Scotland and was nominated for the New York Drama Desk Awards for Outstanding Design for *Hansel and Gretel* (Catherine Wheels).

During Lockdown Karen was one of the founders of the Take a Seat collective. The collective are a group of theatre designers who invited freelance theatre makers to 'take a seat' and make an art work which reflected their situation during lockdown and what they were missing about their work. The project ended in a live installation in the Royal Lyceum Theatre, Edinburgh's glass foyer that was viewed by the public from the street.

Shilpa T-Hyland (Associate Director)

Shilpa graduated from the MA in Classical and Contemporary text at the Royal Conservatoire Scotland in 2017. She has a first-class degree in Theatre Studies and English Literature from Glasgow University and the University of California, Davis.

Recent work as a Director includes: *We'll Meet in Moscow* (Traverse Theatre Company); *Roxana* (Paisley Book Festival/Renfrewshire Leisure); *How to Disappear Completely and Never be Found* (Royal Conservatoire Scotland). Associate Directing work includes: *Pride and Prejudice* (*Sort Of)* (Blood of the Young, Royal Lyceum Theatre, Edinburgh). And as Assistant Director: *Crocodile Fever* (Traverse Theatre Company – JMK regional bursary, funded by the Leverhulme Trust Arts Scholarships Fund).

She was the inaugural winner of the Horsecross Trust Young Director Award, for which she directed a production of *Miss Julie* in February 2019. Upcoming work includes: directing *Revolution Days* (Bijli).

About Traverse Theatre Company

As Scotland's new writing theatre, the Traverse Theatre is a dynamic centre for performance, experience and discovery. Enabling people across society to access and engage with new writing is our fundamental mission.

Our year-round programme bursts with new stories and live performances that challenge, inform and entertain. We empower artists and audiences to make sense of the world today, providing a safe space to question, learn, empathise and – crucially – encounter different people and experiences. We commission, produce and programme for existing and future audiences to offer new and exciting experiences for everyone, and our partnerships with other theatre companies and festivals enable us to present a wide range of innovative performances.

We are passionate about supporting creativity and embracing the unexplored, working with the newest and rawest talent – with an emphasis on the Scottish-based. Through our creative writing programmes we showcase bold art and artists, which is celebrated year round through the performances on our stages and platforms.

The timely, powerful stories that start life on our stages have global impact, resulting in dozens of tours, productions and translations. We are critically acclaimed and recognised the world over for our originality and artistic risk, which we hope will create some of the most talked-about plays, productions, directors, writers and actors for years to come.

Find out more about our work: traverse.co.uk

With thanks

The Traverse Theatre extends grateful thanks to all those who generously support our work, including those who prefer their support to remain anonymous.

Traverse Theatre Supporters
DIAMOND – Alan & Penny Barr, Katie Bradford, Kirsten Lamb, David Rodgers
PLATINUM – Judy & Steve, Angus McLeod, Iain Millar
GOLD – Roger & Angela Allen, Carola Bronte-Stewart, Iona Hamilton
SILVER – Bridget M Stevens, Allan Wilson, Gaby Thomson, Chris & Susan Gifford, Lesley Preston
BRONZE – Barbara Cartwright, Alex Oliver & Duncan Stephen, Patricia Pugh, Beth Thomson, Julia & David Wilson

Trusts, Foundations and Grants
Anderson Anderson & Brown Charitable Initiative
British Council Scotland and Creative Scotland: UK in Japan 2019-20
Dr David Summers Charitable Trust
Garrick Charitable Trust
Harold Hyam Wingate Foundation
Idlewild Trust
John Thaw Foundation
Murdoch Forrest Charitable Trust
The Foyle Foundation
The Great Britain Sasakawa Foundation
The JMK Trust
The JTH Charitable Trust
The Leche Trust
The Mackintosh Foundation
The McGlashan Charitable Trust
The Nancie Massey Charitable Trust
The Nimar Charitable Trust
The Noël Coward Foundation
RKT Harris Charitable Trust
The Robertson Trust
The Royal Edinburgh Military Tattoo
The Russell Trust
The Teale Charitable Trust
The Turtleton Charitable Trust
Unity Theatre Trust
The William Syson Charitable Foundation
The W M Mann Foundation

Traverse Theatre Production Supporters
Cotterell & Co
Paterson SA Hairdressing

Still was written during Frances Poet's Creative Fellowship at the Institute for Advanced Studies in the Humanities (IASH), University of Edinburgh. IASH provides an international, interdisciplinary and autonomous space for discussion and debate. Since its foundation in 1969, more than 1,300 scholars from 70 countries have held Fellowships.

Grant Funders

The Traverse Theatre is funded by Creative Scotland and The City of Edinburgh Council. With additional support from The Scottish Government's Performing Arts Venues Relief Fund, and Adapt & Thrive, part of the Community and Third Sector Recovery Programme, delivered in partnership by Firstport, Corra Foundation, SCVO, Just Enterprise, Community Enterprise and Social Investment Scotland.

Traverse Theatre (Scotland) is a Limited Company (SC076037) and a Scottish Charity (SC002368) with its Registered Office at 10 Cambridge Street, Edinburgh, Scotland, EH1 2ED.

Traverse Theatre

STILL

Frances Poet

For

Daisy Hermione McMorrow 11.09.16
Benjamin McEvoy Collins 06.11.09
Roger Edward Stirk 1939–2012

Acknowledgements

Still exists because I was selected to be the IASH/Traverse Creative Fellow in 2018. Thank you to the panel who chose me, including Ben Fletcher Watson and Orla O'Loughlin, all the IASH team and the many scholars I met through it.

My research was aided by the wonderful Rachel Bradnock, Jennifer Corns and Jen Penman, who sat down with me and shared their professional expertise so generously.

During the play's development, I was lucky enough to mine the brilliant dramaturgical minds of Dominic Hill, Elizabeth Newman and Philip Howard as well as some talented actors: Kenny Blyth, Charlene Boyd, Scott Fletcher, Lesley Hart, Jamie Marie Leary, Fletcher Mathers, Adura Onashile and the 2020 students of the Classic and Contemporary Text course (facilitated by Playwright's Studio, Scotland, Fiona Sturgeon Shea and Marc Silberschatz).

The unflappable and excellent Gareth Nichols has been with *Still* from the beginning and I am so grateful that he chose it to be his first production as AD of the Traverse after the long Covid-19 hiatus. Thank you, Gareth, for so skilfully drawing out the theatricality and joy in the play, assisted by our dependable dramaturg Eleanor White, the musical talent of Ogus Kaplangi, a first-rate creative team, the heroic Traverse staff, and our bloody brilliant cast, Martin Donaghy, Molly Innes, Gerry Mulgrew, Mercy Ojelade and Naomi Stirrat, who all made significant contributions to the play.

Thanks too to Nick Barron, Matt Applewhite and Nick Hern, Cove Park, Helen Matheson, Catherine Wiseman (via my Edinburgh expert, Naomi), my inspiring mummy, Janet Stirk, my big bro, Andrew, and my beloveds: Richard, Elizabeth and especially Peter Poet for his Pokémon expertise.

And finally thank you to my dear friends Lindsay, James, Will, Sam and Jacob McMorrow, and Lucianne, Peter, Grace and Martha Pearl McEvoy Collins.

F.P.

Of pain you could wish only one thing: that it should stop. Nothing in the world was so bad as physical pain. In the face of pain there are no heroes.

George Orwell

I have found the paradox, that if you love until it hurts, there can be no more hurt, only more love.

Mother Teresa

Characters

CIARA, *late twenties/early thirties*
GILLY, *twenties*
DOUGIE, *late twenties/early thirties*
MICK, *sixties*
GAYNOR, *late fifties*

Setting

A space in which five people can exist simultaneously that incorporates a bath/birthing pool. It is Ciara's surgery, Gaynor's home, an NCT meeting room, a palliative care unit, a labour ward, and the pubs and streets of Edinburgh.

This text went to press before the end of rehearsals and so may differ slightly from the play as performed.

1. Exruciating Pain

Friday. A heavily pregnant CIARA *is in her surgery with* GILLY.

GILLY. It's been there quite a while, I suppose. And I tend to be a head-in-the-sand kind of a person at the best of times so I probably should have come a long time ago. And it's pretty gross and I'm not very good with stuff like that so I suppose I hoped it would just sort itself out. But it hasn't. It's grown. It's kind of a… red mushroom coming from the, you know…

She points 'down there'.

CIARA. Okay…

GILLY. It's actually quite pronounced. And it's, well, now it's gone black so…

CIARA. Black?

GILLY. Well a dark sort of… yes, I'd say black.

CIARA. How long has it been black?

GILLY. A few days. Which I don't suppose is a very good thing, is it?

CIARA. And pain?

GILLY. Yes. I didn't… At first… I mean. I've been distracted so… but yes, I'd say quite considerable pain now. Sitting and whatnot. Excruciating pain even.

CIARA. Let's take a look, shall we?

GILLY nods and gets up. Not to remove her trousers – this isn't her consultation. She brings out a small pug from a carry case to her side.

GILLY. Come on, puggywug. This nice lady is going to look at your bits.

CIARA takes the dog.

CIARA. Hello… Puggywug, is it?

GILLY. Mr Immanuel Kant.

CIARA. Sorry?

GILLY. I know, right? It was either that or James Joyce, which would have been no better since she's a girl. Not that my dad could remember that. He has dementia. Lewy bodies. I think he would have called her that even if he had remembered her gender. His sense of humour's always been a bit… She's his pug.

CIARA is examining the pug.

CIARA. What's her appetite like?

GILLY. Not great.

CIARA. Has she been drinking?

GILLY. Not since she joined AA.

Tumbleweed.

Sorry. No, not really. She's never been a big drinker though. Of water.

CIARA finishes her examination.

CIARA. She has a prolapsed vagina.

GILLY. I didn't know that was even a thing.

CIARA. In dogs that aren't neutered it's fairly common. The thing is, we would have hoped to catch this much sooner than we have.

GILLY. But you can make her better?

CIARA. No. I'm sorry.

GILLY. Can't you just cut it out?

CIARA. It's part of her vaginal wall, we can't cut it away. I'm afraid the best thing we can do for her is to put an end to her /

GILLY. No.

CIARA. I know this is hard…

GILLY. I'm taking her home with me. If there's nothing you can do, we'll just go.

GILLY gets up to take her.

CIARA. You can hear her breathing is shallow and she's running a very high temperature. She's septicaemic. She's not getting better from this. And she's in a lot of pain. The kindest thing to do /

CIARA has positioned herself (and her enormous bump) between GILLY and the dog.

GILLY. Can you move please?

CIARA. I can see how important Mr… erm.

GILLY. Mr Immanuel Kant.

CIARA. Yes, it's clear that Mr Iman… Iman–

GILLY. Immanuel Kant.

CIARA. Yes. It's clear that… (*Spit it out CIARA, you can do this.*) *she* is very important to you. And it's hard when you love them so much but ask yourself what you'd want if you were in pain /

GILLY. I am in pain!

She really is. And suddenly it's pouring out of her.

My dad is dying. His swallow has gone. So he's getting no fluids. The doctors say he'll die in days. And now you want to kill his dog too?! Not this week. Please. I need her this week. I can't watch them both die.

CIARA flounders. She's not qualified to deal with this.

CIARA. No. No. Of course not.

GILLY. Is there anything we can do?

CIARA considers.

CIARA. We can push it back in and give her a course of antibiotics. It will be painful and it won't work. But it might buy you a little time.

GILLY. Thank you.

CIARA. Okay.

GILLY. I'll bring her back in. If she's in a lot of pain. I promise. And then you can, you know. End it for her. Just not today.

CIARA. Okay.

GILLY. How do you do it?

CIARA. A wee injection. It's all over in two minutes.

GILLY. So quick. My dad's on day three. Could you give me a dose for him?

CIARA. Not the same for humans.

GILLY. Why not?

CIARA. You can't explain to an animal why they're feeling what they are.

GILLY. Nobody can explain to my dad either. Or if they could, he'd forget. Would I watch as you inject her?

CIARA. It's best. She'll need you to stroke her, talk to her so she can hear your voice.

GILLY. What am I supposed to say to somebody that's dying?

CIARA. Just talk the way you usually do…

GILLY. We haven't talked properly in years. And when he tried to apologise for that, for being shit when my mum died, I didn't understand. He'd bought all this random crap and. Sorry.
I'll ask for you. When I make the appointment.

CIARA *holds her bump*.

CIARA. Last day today.

GILLY. Congratulations. Do you know what you're having?

CIARA. A little girl.

GILLY. Got a name picked out?

CIARA. She's taking my surname so my husband gets to choose.

GILLY. Hope he's a better name-picker than my dad.

CIARA. Me too. No offence…
    My colleagues are great. They'll see you right.

    GILLY *doesn't look convinced.*

2. Portobello Beach

MICK *climbs out of the bath. He's on a beach, wearing yesterday's clothes, which are wet and covered in damp sand. He's disorientated and clutching at his head.*

He focuses enough to take in the audience. He looks at them long and hard. He is confused.

MICK. Where the fuck am I?

3. Still

Saturday morning. GAYNOR *remains absolutely still while* DOUGIE *hurries round her.*

DOUGIE. I couldn't get the cannelloni you like so I got
    tortellini instead. I've crammed about a hundred meals in the
    freezer. M&S's finest – lasagnes, chillis, the lot. I've also
    managed to squeeze one of those six-pint bottles of milk in
    there so even if I can't get back for a while, you'll have milk
    for your tea and your cereal. I know it doesn't taste great
    defrosted. The texture's all… and it looks yellow. Like
    you've scooped up snow that some dog's pissed in…
    anyway, it'll have to do.

    Nothing from GAYNOR.

I'm not saying I won't be in. I'll try but it's uncharted territory, isn't it? I've got loads to tie up at the office and I still haven't chosen a name. When I can, I'll be round. Okay?

Silence.

I'd say it's about now, Mum. That you should say thank you.

GAYNOR *looks up, then out to the audience, whom she addresses.* DOUGIE *does not hear this but waits for his mother to respond.*

GAYNOR. Hang a rat from her tail, she'll struggle to get free. But not for long. Not 'cause she gets comfortable. Gravity pushing blood onto her wee brain, a great pounding pressure. It hurts. But she kens that if she struggles on for too long, she'll die from exhaustion. So she stays still. She saves her energy.

DOUGIE. Mum?

She's back in the room with DOUGIE.

GAYNOR. Thank you.

DOUGIE *waits for something more from her. It doesn't come.*

DOUGIE. Are you having a bad day?

GAYNOR. Not yet 10 a.m.

DOUGIE. You know what I mean. Is it bad?

GAYNOR *throws her response to us. Getting nothing back,* DOUGIE *gives up and returns to clearing away the debris of the shopping he brought.*

GAYNOR *(to us).* I've a throbbing in the back of my neck and between my shoulders. A fire lights up in my right hip if I move so much as a centimetre. There's an earthquake behind my eyes and an ache in the bones of my feet and the inside of my knees like I've walked the earth for a thousand years. I could tell him but it's in my jaw too and the words cost too much.

She's back in the room, responding to DOUGIE.

I'm fine.

DOUGIE. Is your hip still bad?

GAYNOR. Still.

It's unclear whether she's answering him or reminding herself to stay still.

DOUGIE. You seem down… depressed.

GAYNOR. I am.

DOUGIE. So take the antidepressants the doctor gave you. Painkillers might not touch your pain but at least the antidepressants can stop you getting depressed about it.

GAYNOR. I'm okay with depressed.

DOUGIE. You've not left the house in… forever.

GAYNOR. Thirty-one months.

DOUGIE. Jesus and that's okay, is it?

GAYNOR *shrugs.*

Depressed is not okay.

GAYNOR. Seems a sensible response to being in constant pain.

DOUGIE. You've been in pain since I was revising for my Standard Grades. It's not going away. You don't have to live with depression as well.

GAYNOR. They tested antidepressants on rats who /

DOUGIE. Not the rat thing again.

GAYNOR. Hung them from their wee tails and /

DOUGIE. I don't want to hear it.

GAYNOR. They struggled longer when they took the human antidepressants. Struggled until exhaustion killed them.

DOUGIE. You're not a rat. You're a human being. Live like one.

Silence. There's nothing more to say.

Okay, well, I'll see you… on the other side. Hug?

He goes to hug GAYNOR *who, frightened of the pain, pulls away.*

GAYNOR. You always hug too tight.

DOUGIE. Right…

He's waiting for her to say something but GAYNOR *is looking out of the window.*

Are you not going to…? I don't know, Mum. Wish me luck? I'm having a baby. It's a pretty big deal.

GAYNOR. People do it every day.
Ciara'll be grand. Did she not want to pop in with you?

DOUGIE. No, she… she's at home. Resting.

GAYNOR. Home?

DOUGIE. We're going dancing tonight to celebrate her finishing work. I think Ciara's hoping they might even play our song, so we can wow the club with our wedding choreography and her swinging baby-bump curves. We're going to down shots of lime cordial and pretend they're apple sours.

GAYNOR. Ciara's not home, Dougie.

DOUGIE. She is. She's /

A heavily pregnant CIARA *appears.*

CIARA. Sorry to interrupt!

DOUGIE (*quietly to* CIARA). Thought you didn't want to come in.

CIARA. I'm bursting for a pee!

4. Talking is Easy

Friday. GILLY *is by her dad's bedside. Mr Immanuel Kant's animal carrier is beside her and a guitar.*

GILLY. Hi. I'm back. It's me, Gilly.
I think there's a nurse here called Gilly, isn't there? I'm the other Gilly. Your… you know, daughter. God.

Mr Immanuel Kant is here too. She actually looks pretty happy, all snuggled up. The antibiotics must be working.

So. How was your day?

No response. Obviously.

You're getting very good at sleeping. I reckon you could do it with your eyes closed.

Bloody hell, Gilly – is that the best you've got?

What did we used to talk about? When you could have a whole conversation and didn't drift off partway, obsessing about something you'd lost.

Did we ever talk?

We sang. You taught me songs. Ones your dad taught you. Feels a long time ago now.

She absent-mindedly gets out her phone and holds it up.

Bloody hell, Dad, there's a Rayquasa sitting on your head.

5. Thirst

MICK. It's women's screams that wake me up. Three of them in their bikinis running into the North Sea. They look beautiful silhouetted against the rising sun. I think about joining them but it's bitter cold and the whole idea makes me feel like the proverbial hungry squirrel. Concerned for my nuts… I'm not in a good way. Nor would you be if you'd woken up with your head in a salty puddle on Porty Beach. From the taste in my mouth, I must have had a fine old time last night.

I spy a beard in a beanie unlocking a pub.

'Can I beg a drink off you, pal?'

He tells me they don't open for hours but he says it slow like a nurse talking to a brain-damaged patient.

'Aye, I ken that but it's water I want not booze. My mouth tastes like a pug's backside.' Hipster Beard doesn't want to be a dick but he's worried I'm going to sit in his pub all morning, nursing a free drink.

'I'll drink my water, then go,' I promise him. 'I've somewhere I need to be... I just don't remember where the now... And I'm happy to pay.'

I go to get my wallet but...

MICK *puts his hand in his pocket, and the other.*

It's not there. And in its place are... two gold rings.

MICK *holds up the rings, bemused.*

'It's a wedding you're off to, is it?'

'Must be.'

'If you've got the rings, you're either the best man or the groom.'

MICK *knows he's right.*

Oh fuck.

6. My Pain is Scottish

Back in time. Six months ago. CIARA, with no visible baby bump, stands with DOUGIE having just arrived with a delivery of supplies. GAYNOR, her past self more cheerful than the present day GAYNOR we first met (though in no less physical pain), is searching the supplies for something to offer them.

GAYNOR. No biscuits?

DOUGIE. You didn't ask for biscuits.

GAYNOR. Didn't ken you were calling.

DOUGIE. If you're fretting about offering us a biscuit, don't. Neither of us want a biscuit.

CIARA. I do.

GAYNOR *throws a triumphant look at* DOUGIE.

DOUGIE. We don't even need tea. We just want to sit and talk to you a while. Don't look all worried. Just come over here.

GAYNOR *painfully makes her way over.*

CIARA. We've got something to show you.

CIARA *takes out a book from her bag but before she can retrieve something from inside it,* GAYNOR *has taken the book from her.*

It's inside.

GAYNOR. *'Curing Chronic Pain'*?

CIARA. Ignore the book for now. That wasn't what I wanted to show you.

GAYNOR. Naw?

CIARA. My colleague borrowed it from her friend for you but that's not what we're here for.

GAYNOR*'s reading the blurb on the back.*

DOUGIE. Her pal was crippled with fibromyalgia for years and now he runs triathlons most weekends. Says that book saved his life.

GAYNOR *discards the book.*

GAYNOR. Don't have the right trainers to run a triathlon.

DOUGIE. I don't think the running is compulsory. You should read it. The guy doesn't feel any pain at all now.

GAYNOR. Everybody needs some pain. Keeps you safe.

DOUGIE *gives an ironic laugh.*

Folk born without pain gnaw on their tongues like they're chewing the end of a biro. Most of them are dead by their twenties.

CIARA. Can we just forget about the book?

GAYNOR. Thought we'd put an end to friendly advice after that time you called me a bitch.

CIARA. I never called you that!

DOUGIE. She's winding you up.

CIARA. I just said that depressed dogs seem to feel pain more keenly and those with a good attitude healed better. I apologised. Look, I wasn't necessarily even going to pass on the book. Just look inside it, will you.

GAYNOR. Tells you to visualise the pain, does it?

CIARA. I think you're supposed to picture it as an animal, actually. Then you can appraise it objectively and rate your pain levels.

GAYNOR. 'Zero stars. Would not recommend.' How's that for a rating?

CIARA. It's about recognising that you aren't your pain.

GAYNOR. I fucking am. And it's me. And yours is you.

DOUGIE. Except we're not in constant pain.

GAYNOR. Still you though. Your pain is Scottish, male, and it's twenty-nine years old.

DOUGIE. How's my pain any different from anybody else's?

CIARA. Dougie, focus. She might want to read the book when she knows our news…

DOUGIE. If Ciara and I got the same wound on the exact same place on our body, we'd feel it exactly the same.

GAYNOR. Oh aye?

GAYNOR *reaches for* CIARA *and* DOUGIE*'s arms.*

Let me teach you something about experience.

CIARA. What are you doing?

GAYNOR. You're both walking through a wood. Not a care in the world.

CIARA. What's she doing?

GAYNOR. When your arm brushes along a branch and scratches you.

GAYNOR scratches them both.

CIARA. Ow!

GAYNOR. Signals go up to your brain.

CIARA. Gaynor?!

GAYNOR. Brain decides hardly any pain is needed – it's nowt serious. Just a wee scratch.

CIARA. Your mum just scratched me.

DOUGIE. I know. I'm sorry.

GAYNOR. But an hour later, Ciara's body goes into shock. Your scratch was a branch but hers was a snake bite. She nearly dies.

CIARA. Of course the snake would bite me.

DOUGIE. To be fair, if I had a choice between my veiny arm and yours, I'd bite you.

GAYNOR. Her brain feels bad. It under-reacted, delayed her seeking help and nearly paid the ultimate price. Next time you pair go for a walk, could be years later, you're scratched again.

CIARA. Oh no you don't!

CIARA moves away from GAYNOR. She's not taking any chances.

GAYNOR. You, son, feel fine but you, Ciara, you're in agony. 'Danger, danger!' your brain says. The only way it kens how – through pain. 'You ken this feeling. It ended badly last time. Get some help, now!' And even though all you have is a tiny wee scrape on your skin from a branch, your brain will not wheesht. Same cut, same place, but Ciara's experience means she feels it like she's been stabbed with a carving knife.

CIARA. I can't believe you scratched me for that. That really hurt.

GAYNOR. That's 'cause your pain is Scottish too, hen. There's folk on the other side of the world who get brain surgery without so much as a painkiller. Me and pain, we've shared the same life, same culture. We evolve together. I am my pain. And my pain is me. And no amount of picturing it as a cute animal outside of my body is going to stop it.

CIARA. Have you tried?

GAYNOR. I'll tell you what my pain looks like. It's a monstrous mammy. Warning against everything when nothing's broke. She's shriller than a fishwife and the only sound worse is that of folk mouthing off about how to cure me when they don't ken the first thing about it. So if that's what you've come here hoping to do with your self-help pish, you can get to fuck!

She throws the book at them. A small picture drops out of it as she does. Everybody is shell-shocked, including GAYNOR *herself, at the rage that burst out of her.* DOUGIE *picks up the twelve-week baby scan and passes it to her.*

DOUGIE. We didn't. We came to show you this.

GAYNOR *looks*.

GAYNOR. I'm going to be a granny?

CIARA. Not like this you're not.

CIARA *storms out*.

DOUGIE. Bloody hell, Mum.

DOUGIE *gives her a look – disappointment? Pity? He runs after* CIARA. GAYNOR *sits, staring at the photograph.*

7. Charm, Sleep and Psychic Ball

Saturday. GILLY *is by her father's bed. She is playing Pokémon GO on her phone.*

GILLY. So you see I'm using Fairy types to fight the Rayquaza because they're most effective against Dragon types. Which is surprising as this one's as cute as Mr Immanuel Kant and you'd never think she could take on a dragon. But she's got this whole thing she can do adjusting her voice to the brainwaves of her opponent to sing them to sleep. And her singing's got this black-hole quality where she uses up all the air so if anybody tries to resist her, they suffocate. That's mostly background from the cartoon where she's on a quest to get a Moon Stone. On this she's got three moves: Charm, Sleep, and Psychic Ball, and I'm powering her up with Stardust just in case. It's annoying because I'm only three candies away from evolving her up to the next level and then I reckon she could take a Rayquaza easy.

She jabs at the phone as part of the battle.

Come on. One more. Damn it! I lost. I can't claim this Gym now.

She looks between her phone and her dying father. What is she doing?

Sorry.

8. Heart of Midlothian

MICK. I hear the sound of phlegm being sucked up a throat and projectiled before I feel it hit my face.

'Is that you, Mick Walsh?' says the spitter, a grinning man with gappy teeth and ears that sit too high on his head. It's Pat Livingstone! My old school pal, looking as much like a donkey as he ever did.

'Only a tourist would sit on the Heart of Midlothian unless he wanted spat on.'
'I just stopped for a wee rest,' I tell him.

Pat helps me up and I explain about the rings and how I've spent the last two hours visiting every church along Leith Walk and into the city asking who's getting married there the day. I've spoken to a florist, two janies and a minister whose response to me hammering on the manse door so early was far from holy.

'I got no response at St Giles's so I thought I'd sit a while till somebody showed.'

Pat tells me a little luck's all I need and it's spitting not sitting that'll bring me some. He hurls a beauty of a spitball on the stone heart and looks at me expectantly.

MICK *tries to spit, he really tries, contorting his mouth into all sorts of ridiculous shapes, but he doesn't have enough saliva in his mouth. He gives up.*

'You've not turned Hearts supporter since I last knew you?' Pat's looking at me accusingly.

'No, Pat. I just don't have your gift of the gob.'

Pat tells me I need some ale and that he kens the landlady at Nips O'Brandy.

'It's not been called that for decades, Pat.'

'Who cares what it's called if the beer's flowing.'

'I can't. I've no wallet and a wedding venue to find.'

Pat gives me one of his goofiest smiles.

'You must have had quite the bender last night to forget a big thing like a wedding. Do you really not ken who it is you're marrying?'

'Maybe I'm not. It didn't work out too well for me the first time. Maybe I'm best man.'

'Oh I ken who you'd be best man for. Terry Gibson!'

'Terry Gibson punched me in the head on my walk to school every day for seven years. Why on earth would I be his best man, Pat?'

'What's it say on your phone?'

'Battery's dead.'

Pat tells me he can help with that. He's got one of them portable batteries I can borrow while he buys me a pint. Apparently he always carries it so his phone doesn't die when he's in the middle of a battle with a Jigglypuff. And before I've chance to ask him what the fuck is a Jigglypuff, he's pulling me along with him towards the Cowgate.

'Alright, Pat. One wee pint.'

9. Pain is What a Person Says it is

Saturday morning. DOUGIE, GAYNOR *and* CIARA *as in Scene Three.* CIARA *is once again heavily pregnant.*

CIARA. That's not the reason I came in. I wanted to see you, of course. I would have come in anyway. Even if I hadn't needed a pee. I was just having a little rest in the car and then my plan was to /

DOUGIE. Ciara.

CIARA. How are you? Have you had any relief? From the pain.

GAYNOR *addresses us. Oblivious,* CIARA *and* DOUGIE *exchange a look, awkward about the silence.*

GAYNOR. Fifteen years of stabbing pains all over my body. Sound hits me like a hammer to my head. Strong smells can goose me for three days or more. I take a shower and the water skelps me like syringes driven into my skin. I've kenned this pain longer than my son's kenned his wife but still they ask. Is it better yet?

GAYNOR *is back in the room and responds to* CIARA.

No.

CIARA. I might just nip to the loo now, if that's okay?

GAYNOR. Course, hen. On you go.

CIARA *goes.* DOUGIE *knows an explanation is due.*

DOUGIE. She was feeling too tired to come in. Who can blame her? She's thirty-seven weeks pregnant with your grandchild. You didn't even ask how she was.

GAYNOR. She needed a pee.
I'll ask. Course I'll ask.

Silence.

All we can hear is the sound of CIARA *peeing, off. It's a long heavy stream and it's embarrassing that they can both hear it. It finally stops. Relief. Then starts again. A few short bursts and then the chain flushes. Handwashing and then...*

CIARA *returns.*

CIARA. That's better.

GAYNOR *moves to her and puts her hands on* CIARA's *bump without asking.*

Oh.

GAYNOR *moves her hands around the bump without saying a word. It's a bit weird.*

CIARA *makes eyes at* DOUGIE, *who shrugs his shoulders – Don't ask me!* GAYNOR *sees this and, embarrassed, breaks away.*

GAYNOR. You been getting any pain?

Her position makes it look like the question was aimed at DOUGIE.

DOUGIE. Me?!

GAYNOR *runs with it.*

GAYNOR. Some fathers do. Pains, nausea,... weight-gain.

DOUGIE. Are you trying to say I'm getting fat?

GAYNOR *shrugs – Maybe.* DOUGIE *looks at his mum, lost for words.* CIARA *tries to ease things...*

CIARA. I've read about that. Where the dad-to-be lies, all fragile, in a hammock, tended to by all the women, while the new mother delivers the baby then goes straight back to work in the field. Typical men, pretending to feel pain to detract attention from the mum. Don't get any ideas, Dougie.

DOUGIE. Mate at work told me about a tribe that lie the father in the beams above the labouring mother with a cord tied to his balls. The mother pulls it every time she has a contraction. A good tug so he feels what she feels.

CIARA. Now that sounds more like it.

GAYNOR. Folk don't pretend to feel pain.

CIARA. What?

GAYNOR. You said the men 'pretended' to feel pain. Folk don't do that.

CIARA. I…

GAYNOR. Pain is what a person says it is.

CIARA. I didn't mean to, I wasn't saying… I wasn't talking about your pain.

GAYNOR. Never said you were.

DOUGIE. Mum.

GAYNOR. I'm not saying nothing… just pain is what a person says it is. Pisses off all the doctors – the one thing they don't get to be experts about because they can't measure it. Try all they like with their pain scales and lists of words, they can no more measure it than they can measure joy.

CIARA. Okay. We should probably…

GAYNOR. I haven't seen you in so long.

CIARA. Our last NCT session starts soon so…

DOUGIE. Not for an hour.

CIARA. Yeah but. Parking…

GAYNOR. Suits you. The bump. Your skin. Your hair. I ken when I was pregnant with /

CIARA. We need to get going. Sorry.

DOUGIE. I'll get the car.

He goes.

GAYNOR. I didn't mean nothing by all that. Pain is my subject, hen.

CIARA. Oh, I know, Gaynor. I know.

CIARA *goes to leave.*

GAYNOR. When will you bring her to meet me?

CIARA. That isn't how it works, Gaynor. Once she's here, we'll be the ones nested up in our place, receiving visitors and food packages. If you want to meet her any time soon, you're going to have to walk out of your front door.

10. One of the Most Painful Ways to Die

Saturday. GILLY *is on her phone.*

GILLY. I'm not ignoring you. I'm actually googling dying of thirst. So apparently your blood's all thick and sluggish because your temperature's so high without water to cool it down. So your heart's working extra-hard to pump it round your body. And at some point your bladder and urethra will start to burn, your tongue will swell up and your brain will... shrink and tear away from the skull... Says it's one of the most painful ways to die, in fact...

Wow. That was. A mistake.

I read another site that said dying's actually a total buzz. Puts you into a state of mild euphoria. So let's stick with that version, shall we?

I think that's enough Google for today. How about I read you some of my book?

11. Pished

MICK, *six pints down, sings a song with abandon, oblivious to us.*

MICK.

Look at the coffin, with golden handles
Isn't it grand, boys, to be bloody-well dead?

> Let's not have a sniffle, let's have a bloody-good cry
> And always remember: The longer you live
> The sooner you'll bloody-well die.

> Look at the mourners, bloody-great hypocrites
> Isn't it grand, boys, to be bloody-well dead?

He's remembered we're here now and knows an explanation is needed.

Pat used to have a thing with wee Mo so she's agreed to serve us pints until we solve my wedding problem.

Another full pint of Guinness appears in MICK*'s hand. He looks at it with disgust.*

This is number...

He counts on his fingers with difficulty. He hiccups. Sways a little.

Six. And the rest of the pubs in Edinburgh haven't even opened yet. All I want is water. My mouth tastes like somebody's mistaken an oral thermometer for a rectal one. But Mo says you don't get to choose which tap flows in a lock-in.

He gulps at the pint thirstily until it's all gone.

MICK *finishes his song.*

> Let's not have a sniffle, let's have a bloody-good cry
> And always remember: The longer you live
> The sooner you'll bloody-well die!

He sits down.

After an hour telling me the precise difference between a Jigglypuff and a Wigglytuff, Pat's finally applying his brain to my dilemma. It's well-meant but poor old Pat would struggle to spell IQ.
'Tina Campbell. You ken, the one with the pointy tits.'
'I'm not marrying Tina Campbell.'
'How can you be so sure?'
'Because I've not seen her since we took our O-grade Biology exam.'

'*Biology* would be right,' Pat says, giving his balls a good
scratch, 'she was tasty. What about Helen Reilly?'
'No.'
'Tracy Grant?'
'No.'
'Lucy Donaldson?'
'Didn't she die?'
'No?! Are you sure, Mick?'
'I'm sure of nothing, Pat. Until I saw you the day, I thought
you'd died. In a motorbike accident forty years ago.'
'I don't think that was me, Mick.'
'Obviously not, Pat.'

Wee Mo grabs my hand then and tells me she'll search my
palm for answers. Mo's teeth are rotten and her breath stinks
like an old beer cellar but she's got my mother's hands. Same
swollen knuckles with her left index finger a wee bit crooked.

'You've a journey to make today but you won't find where
you're going unless you admit to yourself what you've lost.'

An image steals on me then that makes me almost lose the
breath in my lungs. I don't ken whether it's a memory or a
premonition. A lovely lassie holding up the rings and she's
angry with me. Angry and disappointed and sad. And it hurts
my heart to think of it.

I pull my hands away from Mo's.

'Thanks for the drinks, Mo. Pat. But the first weddings of the
day will be starting soon and I have to get these rings where
they belong even if it kills me.'

'A ring is a symbol of eternity,' Mo slurs. 'You'll find your
end with a beginning.'

It's cryptic bullshit but there's something about Mo. I'm a
scrappy wee boy and I want to coorie-in to her words.

'Thanks, Maw. I mean Mo.' I say as I drag myself out the pub.

A Freudian slip. When you say one thing and mean your
mother.

12. Thanks for the Tortellini

Saturday. GAYNOR *is leaving a message on* DOUGIE'*s answering machine.*

GAYNOR. Hi, son. Think you might still be in your class. You mentioned names and I mind I never emailed you back about inspiration from our family. Maw's sisters were Gladys and Bernice. Think there might have been an Elma on your dad's side. Fuck all inspiration there. If you've any sense you'll wait till you meet her. She'll let you know what she should be called. Och, do what you like. I should learn to shut my gob. You're always giving me hell for not saying enough and then when I do speak, I... Like earlier. Reckon I pissed Ciara off...

Beat.

Hope you're both alright, any road. Enjoy your night out. Not sure about shots but a curry and a pint of Guinness for Ciara should see you right. I'll probably spend my evening in the bath just trying to be still. No need to call back. The ringtone might send me over the edge the day. Thanks again for the tortellini.

She hangs up, cringing at the shit message, looks up at us.

You try leaving a coherent message with a hammer pounding your skull.

13. Worth a Shot

MICK. 'For the last time, Pat, I am not doing the Rose Street Challenge!'

I'm in The Kenilworth. But in my defence the minister at St Giles's laughed in my face and, as Pat pointed out as he trotted behind me like a faithful wee dug, my phone only works when it's connected to his PokeGo battery. It's finally powered up and I'm working through my contacts but Pat keeps buying me pints and it's getting harder to read the names on there.

MICK *makes a call on his mobile, which is attached to a Pokémon GO battery bank.*

'Hello, this is Mick, I'm calling to ask if, well, if you're getting married the day? No? Ken anybody who is?
…I told you who I am. Mick, Mick Walsh. I don't ken who the fuck you are either but there must be some reason I've got your number in my phone. … You're the plumber. Right, well. Sorry to bother you, pal.'

I'm no closer to discovering where I need to be but a rotund blonde, called Queenie, who looks far from regal, has made it her business to make me presentable when I do. She's asking every suit-wearer in the pub if he'll swap clothes with me. Surprisingly few men in suits drink in pubs before lunchtime but Queenie is undaunted.

Magician-like, MICK *conjures a bottle of vodka into his hand.*

'Not vodka, Pat?'
Pat flashes his gappy teeth and says 'It's not always the answer. But it's worth a shot.'
'A shot? You've bought an entire bottle!'

MICK *looks at the vodka, feeling sick at the prospect. He gets out the rings again and looks at them.*

'No. I'm done.'

MICK *detaches his phone from the battery bank and strides out.*

I hear Pat calling after me. 'You can't say no to vodka, Mick. It's forty-per-cent stronger than you!' but I refuse to be distracted from my goal.

He is striding out but, as if on cue, he becomes distracted.

A young lassie with mermaid eyes is sitting silently crying. She can't be more than twenty. She reminds me of somebody but I can't quite put my finger on who. I just ken I can't bear to see her sad. The pal she came in with has her tongue down the throat of some guy she's just met and Mermaid Eyes looks like she's all alone in the world.

'Can I help you, hen?' I ask her.
She says she'll take a drink so I get Pat's vodka and some glasses.

Shot glasses appear.

A smile is starting to form on her pretty wee face as she instructs me to fill four shot glasses to the brim.

MICK *fills four glasses with vodka.*

I guess something about today is making her want to be hungover the morrow. And she's quite forceful about one thing – she refuses to drink alone.

CIARA *takes two of the shot glasses and, as she walks them over to* DOUGIE, *throws out the contents over her shoulder.* DOUGIE *then pours them two shots of lime cordial.* MICK *looks at the remaining two shots, apprehensively.*

DOUGIE *and* CIARA *start hitting their hands on a table like frat boys in a drinking game.*

GILLY *absent-mindedly rocks in her chair by her father's hospital bed, making a banging sound.* GAYNOR *holds her head in her hands and makes a low groan in response to pain.*

CIARA *and* DOUGIE. Down it! Down it! Down it!

Feeling the pressure, MICK *accepts he has no choice but to down the vodka. He holds it up in a toast.* DOUGIE *and* CIARA *hold up their lime-cordial shots.*

MICK.
    I used to ken a clever toast.
    But now I cannot think it.
    So fill your glass to anything.
    And damn your souls, I'll drink it.

He downs his first shot in unison with DOUGIE *and his second with* CIARA. *Spent,* GAYNOR *leans against the side.* GILLY *nearly falls off her chair and, embarrassed, rights herself just in time.*

She's laughing now. And I like this new feeling. Of being useful.

'Alright then, Pat. Line up four more.'

14. Couvade

Saturday, late morning. CIARA *is mid-contraction with* DOUGIE *by her side.* DOUGIE *is watching, fairly dispassionately.* CIARA *is taking lots of deep breaths which are getting shorter as the contraction builds in intensity. Just as the contraction might be expected to reach its climax,* CIARA *stops and turns to* DOUGIE.

CIARA. See.

DOUGIE. Have you finished? I was daydreaming that it was already tonight and we were downing our shots and limbering up for our dance.

CIARA. Somebody can't take constructive criticism.

DOUGIE. It's not an acting exercise.

CIARA. They're asking all the men to simulate a contraction – what is that if it's not an acting exercise?

DOUGIE. It's so we can empathise. With your pain.

CIARA. Can't we just do that whole 'cord round your testicles' thing?

DOUGIE. And even, maybe, so that you can empathise with what it's like to be outside the pain, trying to help but feeling useless.

CIARA. Everybody seems obsessed today with how hard labour can be for men.

Beat.

DOUGIE. I'm sorry my mum's so weird.

CIARA *gives a look – You said it.*

You could pretend you don't hate her.

CIARA. Blame our daughter. If she hadn't rested on my bladder, we could have avoided the whole confrontation.

DOUGIE. Maybe she wants you and her gran to be pals?

CIARA. I think that might take more than a boot to the bladder.

DOUGIE. She might bring us all together.

CIARA*'s not so sure…*

I wish you'd met her before.

CIARA. I like to think the issue your mother has with her nerves isn't the reason she gets on mine.

DOUGIE. She used to laugh.

Beat.

CIARA. Start moaning.

DOUGIE. What?

CIARA. She's looking over at us. We're going to get in trouble.

DOUGIE. Oh God. Okay.

DOUGIE *is about to start but stops…*

I feel inhibited now.

CIARA *gives a moan to show him how.*

CIARA. Aghhhh.

DOUGIE *copies.*

DOUGIE. Aghhhh.

CIARA. Mmmmmmm.

DOUGIE. Mmmmmmm.

CIARA. Uhhhhhhhh.

DOUGIE. Uhhhhhhhh.

15. You Can't Judge a Book by Its Cover

Sunday. The sounds of CIARA *and* DOUGIE*'s moaning carry under* GILLY*'s voice. She is reading her father a trashy romance novel.*

GILLY. 'And she looked into his eyes and she knew. And it was then, without her consciously telling it to, that her hand found its way to his throbbing penis and' oh my God I'm actually reading soft porn to my dying father when I should be reading him something by James Joyce or Henry James or basically anybody with James in their name. Sorry, Dad – I flogged the fancy edition of *Ulysses* you gave for my twenty-first. Let's skip this passage.

She scans ahead.

Actually most of this is pure explicit. Just goes to prove you can't judge a book by its cover. Looked wholesome as hell, all these flowers on it.

She looks at the cover, tilts her head to a different angle.

Nope. Got that wrong too. That should have been a giveaway.

She puts down her book and looks at her guitar.

Maybe a song?

16. Pants Down

CIARA *and* DOUGIE*'s moans bleed into* MICK*'s world.* MICK *wears only his white Y-fronts and white vest. He carries a bottle of Glenfiddich.*

MICK. Sound of a woman moaning pulls me out of the blackness. Must have blanked out again. Is she in pain? Sounds more like ecstasy.

He looks down at his trouserless legs.

Fuck me, I haven't made a woman moan like that in years.

MICK *listens.*

Is that a man moaning too?

He finally sees where the noise is coming from.

I've somehow found my way into a fucking threesome!

I ken now. I agreed to Pat's Rose Street Challenge to cheer up Mermaid Eyes, though she went home with her pal before the fourth pub. In The Abbotsford, Queenie finally found a suit-wearer drunk enough to swap clothes with me. She dragged us both into the disabled toilet and ordered us to strip. That's when things began to turn... amorous.

He sits.

Jesus, I'm thirsty enough to drink the water out of the toilet bowl. But there's two good reasons not to do that. Number one and number two.

Queenie's arse is jutting into my face. Hourglass figure just the sand's shifted a wee bit.

He puts his hands out to caress her imagined buttocks. His face is a mixture of desire and terror. He stops. A smell overwhelms him.

I'm not saying she's wearing too much perfume but if there was a canary in here, I wouldn't fancy its chances.

He vomits. Then looks up.

Sorry! 'As you were. Don't let me stop you.'
Shit, she's pulling him over to me now. He's a fat slug of a man – proper fat, like my old history teacher, Mr Murray, whose rolls of flesh would wibble ironically as he taught us about the great Irish famine. He catches my eye.
'Go on,' he says, 'I want to watch you kiss "the plump mellow yellow smellow melons of her rump".'

MICK *considers.*

'No. No, this isn't for me. Thank you but no thank you. Where are my trousers?'
A vein in Queenie's forehead has started to bulge as she chucks them at my head.

The trousers appear as if by magic and land on MICK. *He holds them out in front of him. They are huge.*

'I need my trousers. The rings are in mine. How can I wear a suit belonging to that fat fucking monster?!'

The Slug doesn't like that. And I'm starting to think there may be more muscle hidden in that hulking body of his than I'd first realised. Oh Christ.

MICK *backs away.*

'What did you say?'
'I called you a fat fuck.'

MICK *claps his hand over his mouth.*

I watch him pull his arm back to get the extra force and now his fist is heading straight for my nose.

In a total change of energy, MICK *steps out of the scene to speak to us.*

Give a man a duck and he's fed for a meal but teach a man to duck...

MICK *steps back and ducks. Yes, the guy missed!*

The force of his missed punch has sent Fat Fuck flailing onto the floor.
'Here's your fucking rings.' Queenie's shoving my gold rings in my hand, her eyes are narrow and her mouth all pursed up like she just got bit by a snake. I ken that look. How didn't I see it before?
'I ken it's you, Theresa. A man never forgets a woman who looks at him with contempt, especially not if he was married to her.'
'I'm not your ex-wife. Jesus, you're more fucked than I realised. You've got a problem with the booze, pal.'
'I've ninety-nine problems but the booze ain't one.'

He looks to us – are we judging him?!

I'm not an alcoholic, if that's what you think. They go to meetings. Drunks go to parties!

MICK, *rings in hand, scoops up the suit and, whisky bottle held aloft, stumbles off in his pants.*

17. Singing and Dancing

Monday. GILLY *finishes tuning her guitar. There's no more procrastinating. She's going to have to play something. She starts to hum and slowly begins to find the words.*

GILLY (*singing*).

    The night Pat Murphy died is a night I'll never forget
    Everyone got roarin' drunk and some not sober yet;
    As long as the bottle was passed around and everyone
        feeling gay
    O'Leary came with bagpipes and music for to play.

She finds the chords on the guitar and starts to sing with much more confidence.

    Mrs Murphy sat in the corner, pourin' out her grief
    While Kelly and his friends, those dirty, robbin' thieves
    They crept into the anteroom and a bottle of whisky stole
    They placed the bottle on the corpse to keep the liquor
        cold.

Her voice is mic'd now. The sound is big and raucous and like a gig in a pub.

    And that's how they showed their respect for Paddy
        Murphy
    That's how they showed their honour and their pride.

MICK, *trousers still draped over his arm, wanders across the stage as if he's just stepped into a new pub.*

MICK. Best pub yet. Can't beat live music. What a voice! What a tune!

MICK *joins in with the chorus, his bottle of whisky in hand.*

GILLY *and* MICK (*singing*).

    They said it was a sin and a shame and they winked at one
        another

Now everything in the wakehouse went, the night Pat
Murphy died.

CIARA *and* DOUGIE *dance along. A gloriously silly
choreographed dance they learnt for their wedding day that
is made all the funnier and more glorious because of*
CIARA*'s giant bump.*

At three o'clock in the morning, some dirty blue-eyed
scamp
He wrote upon the coffin lid, 'Herein lies a tramp,'
They stopped the clock so Mrs Murphy couldn't tell the
time
And at a quarter after three, sure they told her it was nine.

MICK *clambers onto the edge of the bath, balancing,
dancing, singing and drinking.* GAYNOR*'s swaying in pain
but even that feels timed to the music.*

And that's how they showed their respect for Paddy
Murphy
That's how they showed their honour and their pride;
They said it was a sin and a shame and they winked at one
another
Now everything in the wakehouse went, the night Pat
Murphy died.
At eight o'clock in the morning,
The funeral left the house
And everyone but poor ol' Mrs Murphy was out soused
They stopped on the way to the churchyard at the old
Red-Door Saloon
They went in there at nine o'clock
And they didn't come out till noon.

*At the height of the song, still balancing precariously on the
bath,* MICK*'s had a revelation.*

MICK. I remember. I remember!

And he promptly falls into the bath – splash.

And as quickly as it started, it's over. CIARA *and* DOUGIE
have abandoned the dance. GAYNOR*'s locked into her pain.*

And GILLY *is no longer mic'd. She sings the last verse
quietly and with much less gusto by her father's bed.*

GILLY (*singing*).
Someone asked ol' Finnegan if anyone had died
'Lou,' says he, 'I'm not quite sure, I just came for the
ride.'
They started out for the graveyard all in a very straight
line
But when they reached the grave, they found they'd left
the corpse behind.

GILLY *has finished the song. What now?*

I didn't think you'd hold on so long, Dad.

They say it'll be soon. I'm allowed to make up a bed here
tonight if I want. Apparently it's an incredible privilege for
me to be able to sit in this room with you. Most people
would be grateful. But I... I don't know. I'm just so tired.

18. The Beginning

CIARA *emerges from a birthing pool. She's having a
contraction but it's early stages.* DOUGIE *has his nose in a
baby-name book.*

CIARA. Another one's coming.

DOUGIE. Another one? Shit. That's less than ten minutes.
They're getting closer and I still haven't chosen a name!

CIARA*'s contraction is building...*

CIARA. If don't you start rubbing my back, I'll shove that
baby-name book so far down your throat, you'll have to give
birth to it.

CIARA*'s contraction builds and she disappears into the
bath.* DOUGIE *discards the book and goes towards her but*
GAYNOR*'s in the way. She's standing right in front of him
and watches him step round her and climb into the bath after*
CIARA.

19. Mother's Intuition

GAYNOR*'s still standing by the bath.*

GAYNOR. Dougie.

My lad's face vivid as if he was standing in front of me.

I used to be intuitive. I'd ken something big had happened to him even if I wasn't with him: a fight in the school playground, that time he won the Mastermind Trophy. I'd ken without him even needing to tell me. The pain pushed all that out. But I feel it now. I feel him. As vividly as a blade cutting into skin.

GAYNOR *gets her phone and leaves* DOUGIE *another message.*

Dougie, strangest thing. I'd cry it mother's intuition but I'm not sure you'd credit me with that. Ciara's birthing my granddaughter now. I'd stake my life on it. Maybe she's here already. Call me. Any time. Don't worry about the noise. I'll manage.

She hangs up.

I mind it now. What it felt like to birth my son. His spine rubbing against my own because he forgot to turn. The pressure on my thighs and lower back so intense, I shook with it. And then he arrived. Face up, I'm told, and he's passed to me and the pain… just. Stopped. Just like that. I held my boy and my torn and bruised body melted away into nothing.

I want to hold my grandchild.

All I need to do is step out of my front door.

20. I Ken

MICK *drags himself out of the bath, determined.*

MICK. I ken who Mermaid Eyes reminded me of. My daughter. My sweetheart. I thought she was still that little tot who I sing songs with in the bath but she's… she's a grown woman now. How could I forget a thing like that?

It's not her wedding day, is it? Am I supposed to be walking my daughter down the aisle?

21. My Body Minds How It Felt Last Time

GAYNOR. But I can't. Course I can't. Because my body minds how it felt last time. A bucket of ice chucked in my coupon when I step into the air. Nails driven into the soles of my feet each step I take. The rough upholstery of the bus seat scratching into my thighs if I even get that far.

22. My Sweetheart

MICK. She lost her mum. I'm all she has now.

23. Stepping Out

GAYNOR. Folk say you can trick a brain. Placebo power. My uncle told me stories of American soldiers in World War Two who stopped screaming in agony when they got shots of saline, never kenning the morphine had run out long ago. I'm going to stand up and it'll feel better.

She stands. GILLY *and* MICK *stand at the same time.*

GILLY. I think I'm going to go home, Dad. I'm sorry, I just can't…

MICK. I need to find her. I mustn't let her down.

GAYNOR. I'm going to step out that door and enjoy the cold air, the feeling of concrete under my feet, the bumps and jolts on the bus. And you, pain, you can piss off.

MICK *pulls on the oversized trousers while making his way across the stage. The route he takes means the other characters become obstacles. But he's determined.*

MICK. Don't try to stop me. I've had a perfect day but today wasn't it.

GAYNOR. You're outside of me. Just like the books say. You're no monstrous mammy. Just a sorry wee pug that doesn't want to go out into the rain. Well I've got your leash and I'm telling you we're going.

MICK's managed to tie a knot in the belt to secure the huge trousers. The enormous shirt and suit jacket swamp him but he's making an effort to get the tie just right.

GILLY. Let go if you want to. Don't wait for me. You could just slip away…

She looks at him and knows this might be the last time she sees him alive. All three of them step out.

MICK. The pub's behind me now and Princess Street's ahead. I see a bus and I ken it's the one I need. I can't let it go without me. I move faster than I have in years, trying to catch the eye of the driver so he waits for me. I'm going to make it. I'm going to… Fuck!

A screech of tyres.

24. Worlds Collide

Monday. On the street.

GILLY. What are you doing?

GAYNOR. The bus – don't let it go without me.

GILLY. I nearly killed you and you're worried about the bus?

GAYNOR. I need to get to the hospital.

GILLY. Are you okay? Are you in pain?

GAYNOR. Yes. But shhh, don't tell my brain that.

GILLY. Sorry?

GAYNOR. My son and his wife are having a baby.

GILLY. Okay?

GAYNOR. I don't ken that for sure but I had the strongest feeling. And he hasn't answered my calls. There are some things you ken you can't miss. Or you'll regret it forever…

GILLY. Yeah. I get that.

Beat.

I'll take you. To the hospital.

GAYNOR. But you were going in the other direction?

GILLY. I was but… I shouldn't have been. I'll take you.

25. Trust in the Wasp

MICK. I'm a nose away from an ugly yellow-and-black motorcycle and sidecar that screeched to a halt just in time. The driver, a fella of ages with me, wearing a bright-lemon jumper that matches his bike, takes off his helmet and grins like he didn't just near kill me.

(*Irish accent.*) 'Thought I might find you here!' he says 'Get up, lad.'
'Do you ken me?' I ask him.

'I've never met a man I haven't liked more for having a few drinks in him but if you're asking me that, I'd say you've had one too many, son.'

There's something pure familiar about the way his skin dimples when he grins.

'Get in,' he says and he points at the tiny sidecar, 'we've a ceremony to go to. You still got them?'

'The rings? Aye. Will we get there in time?' I ask.

'Trust in the Wasp, son.'

26. Black Hole

GAYNOR *reaches* DOUGIE, *who is holding a jug of water he had a nurse refill.*

GAYNOR. Dougie!

DOUGIE. What are you doing here?

GAYNOR. Am I a granny yet?

DOUGIE. What?

GAYNOR. You told me what hospital and I just had this sense it was now. That she was coming now and I... I pushed the pain outside of me like the books say and I talked to it and I told it that it wasn't going to stop me seeing my first grandchild and... here I am. How's Ciara doing?

DOUGIE. She's... (*Holding up the jug.*) thirsty. Contractions are pretty close now. I need to get back.

DOUGIE *starts to go*.

GAYNOR. Course. I'll wait here until she's born.

DOUGIE *stops*.

DOUGIE. You've shown no interest. None. And now when... now you're excited?

GAYNOR. Of course I'm excited. I want to meet my wee granddaughter.

DOUGIE *looks winded*.

DOUGIE. She's...

GAYNOR. Is everything alright?

CIARA *is sitting. A memory, which* DOUGIE *walks in to join*.

CIARA. I didn't want to bother you at the office and I'd felt fine this morning at the NCT class but as soon as I thought of it, I got this horrible sinking feeling and Kerry's moaning on about Sam and we'd ordered cake that still hadn't arrived but I couldn't shake the feeling and I just wanted reassurance so I made up an excuse and came here and um. They didn't see me straight away because it's quite busy. There's a woman giving birth to triplets apparently. But then this nice midwife

came and we chatted about colours… she liked my top and I told her we'd chosen a similar colour for the baby's bedroom. And she's holding the Doppler over my tummy and she's talking about the colour she chose for her living room – Farrow and Ball do this really nice but expensive shade of green but she found the exact same colour… I don't know where. Because she doesn't finish the sentence. And the colour has drained from her face because there's no… you know. And she tells me she's going get the consultant. And then this nice lady comes in wheeling a scanner. And she holds the probe to my bump and after a few minutes she takes my hand and tells me…
She's dead.

DOUGIE. No.

CIARA. Yes.

DOUGIE. No.

CIARA. I'm sorry. I'm sorry. I'm sorry.

DOUGIE. Are they sure? How can they be sure?

CIARA. There's no heartbeat. She isn't moving. There's no blood coming in or out of the placenta. She's…

DOUGIE. This isn't…

CIARA. I'm sorry.

DOUGIE. Don't be sorry.

CIARA. We were going to go dancing.

DOUGIE. Yeah.

CIARA. No dancing then.

DOUGIE. No dancing.

We're back with GAYNOR *now.*

GAYNOR. On Saturday? It's Monday the day.

DOUGIE *is forced to leave* CIARA *to rejoin his mother.*

DOUGIE. They gave Ciara something to start things off and sent us home. Had to sit there pretending to watch the telly, Ciara stroking her bump, like everything was normal. Just waiting.

GAYNOR. Can I see Ciara?

DOUGIE. No. I don't think that's a /

GAYNOR. No?

DOUGIE. You make her feel uncomfortable, Mum.

GAYNOR. Because I scratched her that time.

DOUGIE. It's not just that. Take Saturday. You were so weird with her. You didn't ask about her. You just touched. You put your hands on her. All that talk about /

GAYNOR. I didn't hurt her.

DOUGIE. I'm not saying /

GAYNOR. You think it was me touching her?

DOUGIE. No, I... Fuck's sake, Mum. I didn't mean... I wasn't... This isn't about you. You're a black hole, Mum. Everything gets drawn into your orbit. You suck the life and joy out of... Maybe it was. Maybe it was you. You touched my baby and her little heart stopped. And now Ciara has to, now we have to...

Destroyed, DOUGIE *walks away from his mother.*

27. Labour Pains

Monday. GILLY *walks back to her father's bedside.*

GILLY. I'm here, Dad. I came back. Don't know if you know either way but... I'm here.
I just met a woman who's a /

GAYNOR. Black hole.

GILLY. Pure expert on pain.
She said even if you could speak, you'd struggle to explain what you're feeling.

GAYNOR. Nobody kens you.

GILLY. Apparently doctors have these pain scales to try to understand. A list of words.

GAYNOR. Words don't work. I could describe you till the end of time, they'll never see you.

GILLY *looks up the McGill pain scale on her phone.*

GILLY. Flickering.
Quivering.
Pulsing.

CIARA *cries out in pain.*

GAYNOR. Throbbing.
Beating.
Pounding.

DOUGIE. Bad one?

CIARA *nods.*

GILLY. Flashing.

GAYNOR. Jumping.

GILLY. Shooting. Is that what it feels like, Dad? The pain?

DOUGIE. It's okay. You're doing great.

MICK. I'm not feeling too good. Not good at all.

GAYNOR. Pricking.

GILLY. Boring.

GAYNOR. Drilling.

CIARA *calls out in pain.*

DOUGIE. Oh, sweetheart.

MICK. I'm on my way to you, sweetheart.

GILLY. Stabbing.

GAYNOR. Lancinating.

GILLY. Smarting.

DOUGIE. Let's get you something. To take away the pain.

CIARA. Why?

DOUGIE. So it doesn't hurt.

CIARA. Everything about this pregnancy has hurt.

GAYNOR. Cutting.

GILLY. Lacerating.

GAYNOR. Pinching.

GILLY. Pressing.

GAYNOR. Gnawing.

GILLY. Cramping.

GAYNOR. Tugging.

DOUGIE. This doesn't have to. They can blast you with
    pethidine so you don't feel a thing. That's the one upside. It
    won't effect her.

GILLY. Pulling.

GAYNOR. Searing.

GILLY. Stinging.

CIARA. No. I want to feel it.

GAYNOR. Wrenching.
    Aching.
    Crushing.

28. Warrington Cemetery

MICK *is wearing a ridiculous sixties helmet and jigging around
in his seat.*

MICK. I'm hurtling down Dundas Street in a metal sidecar
    positioned so low to the ground my head's at car-exhaust
    height. I'm trying my best to disprove my body's theory that

adrenalin is brown. My friend in the yellow jumper cuts it so close on a roundabout we nearly crash into a silver Mercedes. He just laughs. 'I've always wanted to know if a Mercedes bends.' I still don't ken where we're headed but we're moving towards where I started my day.

'Think you're escaping and run into yourself. Longest way round is the shortest way home.'

When he finally stops, it's not at a church but at a cemetery and he's walking us towards a group of mourners gathered around a coffin.

MICK *takes off his helmet.*

'Thought you were bringing me to a wedding?'

'Ceremony I said. Don't look so disappointed. Why, doesn't "funeral" have the word "fun" in it after all!' And he laughs and I don't ken how I didn't see it before.

'You look like my da.'
'I am your da, you silly wee fucker,' he says.
'But you're dead,' I say.
'That I am, lad, that I am.'
'Is this your funeral?' I ask him.
'No, son,' he says, 'it's yours.'

I laugh but he's not laughing back.

I walk through the assembled mourners toward the coffin and I ken every single coupon that looks up at me. My obese history teacher, Mr Murray, who is the very last man on earth I'd choose to be in a threesome with, and my disappointed ex-wife Theresa, who I once promised to treat like a queen. My old maw with her swollen knuckles, known to her pals as Mo. And dear old Pat, with the donkey ears, who gave me my first taste of mortality when he died in a motorbike accident in his twenties.

I've spent the day drinking with the dead. Oh fuck. And the rings in my pocket are no longer little rings of eternity. They're broken. A section of gold missing in each. And I feel…

MICK is no longer the gregarious raconteur. He's a frightened little boy.

'I don't like it, Da. I don't like it at all. I want to go home.'
'You can't go home, lad,' Da tells me, 'time's up.'
'It can't be. I've somewhere I need to be. What about the rings?!'
'The earrings, you mean. A gift,' he says, 'for your daughter.'
My wee Gilly.
(*Panicked now.*) I need her. Gilly! I need to see her face.

29. Worlds Collide Again

Monday. GILLY, by her dad's bedside, has seen him open his eyes.

GILLY. Dad? Can you hear me?

She shouts to a member of the nursing staff, off.

His eyes are open.
Dad, I'm here.

MICK's breathing is laboured now. He is bound by his body for the first time in the play. His dying body. He breathes deep heavy breaths, all the time not taking his eyes off GILLY.

MICK. –

GILLY. Hi, Dad. What do I…? Do you want me to read or… or sing or…

MICK sees GILLY is wearing the earrings. He might even manage to point at them.

MICK. –

GILLY. I'm wearing them. I'm sorry I shouted when you gave them to me. You were just confused and spending money, more than either of us have, on random stuff, and I knew things couldn't continue and I was going to have to put you in a home. I didn't realise you meant them for me. That you were trying to say sorry. About Mum. About letting me down. You haven't let me down, Dad. Dad?

30. Labouring

MICK*'s back with us.*

MICK. I haven't let her down.

That's what MICK *was searching for. It brings him peace.*

I'd better be getting in the coffin, I suppose. If it's to be my funeral.

I slide off the lid but there's no bottom to it, just an empty hole going down and down and down. Oh hell.

Nah. I don't fancy that. There must be another way. And I'm wracking my brains for what it might be when a red-and-white ball cracks against my skull. I pick it up. It's got a white circle in the centre and I'm trying to work out what's familiar about it when I see another one heading straight for my face. I manage to dodge it and run behind a cluster of trees but the balls are coming thick and fast now. Thrown by people I don't recognise who are climbing out of the coffin and trying to catch me. I ken what this is. I'm a fucking Jigglypuff!

Now I've learnt a thing or two about HokePokémon. An Igglybuff becomes a Jigglypuff when it reaches a certain point of happiness but it takes something else for it to level up to the top of the evolution tree. I just dinnae ken what. Was it Stardust or a Moon Stone?

There's a huge Douglas fir behind me that looks tall enough to reach the stars and the moon and I throw myself onto it. There's no footholds and the bark's tearing into the skin of my hands. I feel myself sliding back down it, all the while having Poké Balls thrown at me.

GILLY. You're doing so well.

MICK. Pat's voice and he's launching something at me. Candies! Three of them. Exactly the number I need. And I gobble them down and it's like I'm drinking the freshest spring water ever tasted and my thirst is quenched at last. And I find a purchase in the bark of the tree and within minutes I'm up into the branches and the Poké Balls can't get me here.

GILLY. Not much longer, Dad. Nearly there.

MICK. The tree stretches out higher than the clouds and I ken I have to keep climbing if I want to feel the sun on my skin.

DOUGIE. You can do it.

CIARA. Agggggh.

DOUGIE. Ten centimetres, sweetheart. You're so close. It'll soon be over.

CIARA. And then what?!

DOUGIE. Don't think about that.

GILLY. Let go, Daddy. Just let go. It's okay.

DOUGIE. You're so nearly there.

MICK. I feel heavy as earth but I'm heaving myself up, inch by inch. I still can't see the top of the tree but it's bright up there and I can hear the sounds of old friends.

CIARA. Is she coming?

DOUGIE. I can see her little head.

MICK. I climb and I climb.

GILLY *and* DOUGIE. You're nearly there. You're doing so well.

MICK. And I climb and I climb.

CIARA. She's coming.

MICK. And I climb and I climb.

DOUGIE. One last push.

GILLY *and* DOUGIE. I'm here.

    CIARA *pushes*.

CIARA. Huuuuuuuuuuh.

MICK. And I climb and I /

    He stops.

    It's over.

MICK *has died.*

DOUGIE. You did it. She's here.

CIARA. What does she look like?

DOUGIE. Oh my God, Ciara, she's so beautiful.

CIARA. Let me see her.

GILLY. Dad?

They hold their baby.

CIARA. My little stillborn girl. She is… everything.

DOUGIE. Isn't she just.

CIARA. She looks like you. Around the eyes.

DOUGIE. She's got your chin.

CIARA. And my hair.

DOUGIE. Yes. Look at her tiny fingers.

CIARA. She's… perfect.

GILLY. It's done now, Dad. No more pain.
    Go well.

DOUGIE. I ken her name. Just needed to see her first.

CIARA. And?

DOUGIE. Joy.
    What do you think?

31. Bambi and the Rat

Wednesday. GAYNOR *is in the bath.*

GAYNOR. They tell me to ignore you. To go out and live my
    life. And look what happens. The world outside my door
    isn't made for stillness. I'm like a deer that's learnt to freeze
    when I sense a wolf. In the right environment, I'm a
    survivor. It's only if they force me out onto a road in front of
    headlights that my stillness will get me killed!

Who am I kidding? Bambi's no different from the rat hanging from its tail. They're both fucked. Stillness always leads to death eventually.

She sinks under the water.

32. Goodbye, Mr Immanuel Kant

Wednesday. CIARA's surgery. Mr Immanuel Kant is resting on a table, being stroked by GILLY. CIARA is preparing a needle with a pink-coloured pentobarbital.

GILLY. This is so kind of you.

CIARA. All appointments get automatically emailed to my calendar. And when your name pinged up, I just… I felt it should be me.
I wanted to ask after your dad. Did you talk to him?

GILLY. No. I was shit.
I was there though. When he died. I nearly wasn't but then I almost killed a woman and I… I went back.

CIARA. That's good. Not the 'almost killing someone' bit. That you were there.

GILLY *touches her earrings.*

GILLY. Yeah.

Beat.

The receptionist told me about…

GILLY *points to CIARA's absent bump.*

CIARA. They're going to send an email round so I don't have to keep explaining to everybody but they weren't expecting me in so soon. I wasn't expecting me in so soon.

GILLY. I'm really sorry.

CIARA. It'll be easier when everybody forgets I was pregnant.

Beat.

GILLY. Did you take pictures?

The 'Poorly Pug' website I found said… they call them paw-traits, which is cheesy but kind of cute so I've been taking lots. I've uploaded them to a printing service so now I'm just… Snow White waiting for her prints to come. I mean obviously it's totally different… pugs are not… You can tell how bad my photos are going to be – I can't even stay focused in this conversation.

CIARA. My husband had some printed into an album within hours. But who wants to look at something like that?

GILLY. I would.

Did he choose her a name?

CIARA. Not one that fits.

I counted eight prams on my way to work. Every one feels like being scratched. But worse because my body remembers the snake bite.

GILLY. Are you sure you should be working?

CIARA. Once I've looked after Mr Immanuel Kant, I'll go home. Where my husband will ask me how I am twenty times an hour. That makes me sound like a total bitch.

GILLY. Nah. Sometimes words cost too much. Could go somewhere else. A walk maybe?

CIARA. I'd rather be still.

The needle is ready. GILLY *knows it's time to say goodbye to Mr Immanuel Kant.*

GILLY. Do you need me to step away?

CIARA. No, that's why we put in the IV line. So you can be the one to hold her.

GILLY. I shouldn't have made her wait. But she's seemed okay mostly. Purr-grunting during cuddles like she normally does. Nuzzling up to me. Until late last night.

CIARA. This will take away her pain.

An acknowledgement from these two women in pain that this is the only course of action.

GILLY. You said I should talk to her, while… Do you mind if I sing instead?

CIARA. Whatever makes her happy and calm.

GILLY. She likes this one. My dad used to sing it to her.

CIARA *gives* GILLY *the nod to start singing her goodbye song for her beloved pug.*

(*Singing.*)
 Now Delaney had a donkey that everyone admired
 Temporarily lazy and permanently tired
 A leg at every corner balancing his head
 And a tail to let you know which end he wanted to be fed.

Having moved towards the pug with the needle, CIARA *now steps out of the scene while* GILLY *sings on.*

 Riley slyly said, 'We've underrated it, why not train it?'
 Then they took a rag
 They rubbed it, scrubbed it, they oiled and embrocated it
 Got it at the post and when the starter dropped the flag
 There was Riley pushin' it, shovin' it, shushin' it
 Hogan, Logan and everyone in town.

CIARA *moves towards the bath and stands over it until* GAYNOR *splutters out of the water. She wraps a towel around her and climbs out with difficulty.* CIARA *reaches out her hand to help.* GAYNOR *keeps hold of it and, when she's safely out, kisses it.*

 Lined up, attackin' it and shovin' it and smackin' it
 They might as well have tried to push the town hall down.
 The donkey was eyein' them, openly defyin' them
 Winkin', blinkin' and twistin' out of place
 Riley reversin' it, everybody cursin' it
 The day Delaney's donkey ran the half-mile race.

GILLY *leaves the vets.*

CIARA *and* GAYNOR *sit down next to each other. Still.*

33. Every Last Painful Bit of It

Wednesday. DOUGIE *enters and puts supplies away in*
GAYNOR's *fridge.* GAYNOR, *now wearing a dressing gown,*
moves to him.

GAYNOR. I wasn't expecting you.

DOUGIE. I know it's late. I brought you milk.

GAYNOR. You didn't need to.

DOUGIE. The frozen stuff's awful and you must be out of fresh
by now. Unless you've been out again?

   GAYNOR *shakes her head.*

So I did need to.

   A silence.

You've nothing you want to say to me?

GAYNOR. What do you want me to say?

DOUGIE. It's so dark in here.

GAYNOR. I'll turn on the lights.

DOUGIE. Won't make any difference. I can't find Ciara.

   GAYNOR *turns to look back at where* CIARA *now lies,*
   sleeping. DOUGIE *doesn't see.*

She won't speak to me. I mean she'll do anything to not
speak to me. She went into work this morning, for fuck's
sake. Even forgetting what we've just been through, she's a
mess physically. Still bleeding and leaking milk. But she
heads out the door like it isn't total insanity. Apparently she
put down some pug and walked out before lunch and didn't
come back. I've been everywhere. She's not with friends, her
dad's not seen her. She's barely slept since Saturday and I'm
worried that /

GAYNOR. She's here.

DOUGIE. Here?

GAYNOR. Asleep on my bed.

DOUGIE. She came to you?!

GAYNOR. Buzzed on my door at around noon.

DOUGIE. What did she say?

GAYNOR. Nowt. Just sat next to me. Still.

DOUGIE. For ten hours?

GAYNOR. Till she fell asleep.

> DOUGIE *processes this, makes a decision.*

DOUGIE. I'm going to wake her.

GAYNOR. Let her be.

DOUGIE. I don't want her here.

GAYNOR. She's fine.

DOUGIE. She is far from fine and this the very last place she needs to be. It's like cheering up a lemming by taking her for a walk on a cliff. No. She needs to come home.

GAYNOR. She chose to be here.

DOUGIE. That's what worries me. No well person would choose this.

> *Beat.*

GAYNOR. Because I'm a black hole?

DOUGIE. I'm not even sorry I said it, Mum. It's true. The things you've said to me. 'Life is pain, son.' Fifteen years old, you told me that. Every choice I've made has been to escape and find the… the lightness. Ciara is full of it. Or she was. I've tried to bring that light to you but you are a pure expert at pushing it away. And now, this… thing has happened. To me. And to Ciara. And maybe I could deal with it if I hadn't spent so many years with you but I've no defences left. I feel myself being sucked in. Scares the shit out of me, Mum. That everything you've taught me could be true because, in your shoes, I wouldn't take one pill, I'd take the whole fucking bottle.

So unless you can take it back, find something, anything, hopeful to share with me, I can't... with you... I'm done.

GAYNOR*'s trying. Really trying but the words won't come.*

I'm getting Ciara.

He's heading off towards CIARA. GAYNOR *calls after him.*

GAYNOR. Colic.

DOUGIE. What?

GAYNOR. I wish she'd had it. Your wee girl.

DOUGIE. What the fuck?!

GAYNOR. Her wee tummy bloating with it. Straining to push her waste down tiny tubes that haven't been used before. And tender inflamed gums with sharp wee teeth tearing through them so that her whole mouth feels raw with it.

DOUGIE. This is... What are you saying?

GAYNOR. And being so tired that her head aches and her eyes are sore with crying. And the dull ache on her bruised bumped head when she falls after trying to walk by herself. And the scratch of gravel on her knee when she falls off the tricyle at nursery. The shin splints when she's running at school. The belly ache from eating too many sweeties at her birthday party. The growing pains as her body stretches longer and longer. The cramps of her first period. The itch of the hickey on her neck. The tearing tightness of her 'first time'. The deep physical agony of her first heartbreak. I wish she'd felt it all. Every last painful bit of it. I wish she'd lived.

DOUGIE *is overwhelmed. She did it. Brought her world view in line with his. He doesn't need to battle the darkness now. He can accept it is part of the light. His response is part laughter, part tears, part recognition. They laugh/cry together. It lasts a long time until...*

DOUGIE. I wish you'd live.

GAYNOR. I am. I will.
Come here.

*She opens her arms and he goes to her. He squeezes her
tight. She winces. He's hurt her but she doesn't want to say.*

DOUGIE. Too tight?

GAYNOR. No. It's perfect.

34. Goodbye, Dad

GILLY *is sitting on Arthur's Seat holding an urn.*

GILLY. I reckon this is the spot, Dad. You can see the whole
city and beyond. Porty Beach, Leith Walk, St Giles's,
Cowgate, Rose Street and all your old haunts.

I'm not going to make a big speech. You know I'm shit at all
that. Always have been. But I did want to say one thing. I've
had time to think about it and… it was a privilege to be with
you at the end. Thanks for waiting for me.

Bye, Dad.

GILLY *scatters* MICK's *ashes. They swirl like a tornado,
from which* MICK *emerges.*

MICK. Fuck me, what I wouldn't give to breathe just one more
breath.

35. Joy

CIARA *tentatively opens the album of the photos of her little girl.
It scares her but she relaxes once she starts to look at the images.*

CIARA. I'm holding you, baby. Even though it hurts like I'm
holding fire, I'll tell my brain that it's got it wrong. You're
not pain, little one. You're joy. My Joy.

Blackout.

The End.

A Nick Hern Book

Still first published in Great Britain in 2021 as a paperback original by Nick Hern Books Limited, The Glasshouse, 49a Goldhawk Road, London W12 8QP, in association with the Traverse Theatre, Edinburgh

Cover image: Mihaela Bodlovic

Designed and typeset by Nick Hern Books, London
Printed in the UK by Mimeo Ltd, Huntingdon, Cambridgeshire PE29 6XX

A CIP catalogue record for this book is available from the British Library

ISBN 978 1 83904 027 6

www.nickhernbooks.co.uk

facebook.com/nickhernbooks

twitter.com/nickhernbooks